Lerner SPORTS

ALL-STAR
SMACK
DOWN

# TOM BRADY VS. JOE MONTANA

## WHO WOULD WIN?

DAVID STABLER

D1736789

Lerner Publications ◆ Minneapolis

SPORTS THRILLS *MEET* RESEARCH SKILLS

Lerner SPORTS

Free Database Trial: **lernersports.com**

Lerner Publications Company
An imprint of Lerner Publishing Group, Inc.
241 First Avenue North
Minneapolis, MN 55401 USA

For reading levels and more information, look up this title at www.lernerbooks.com.

Main body text set in Aptifer Sans LT Pro.
Typeface provided by Linotype AG.


**Library of Congress Cataloging-in-Publication Data**

Names: Stabler, David author.
Title: Tom Brady vs. Joe Montana : who would win? / David Stabler.
Other titles: Tom Brady versus Joe Montana
Description: Minneapolis, MN : Lerner Publications, [2024] | Series: All-star smackdown. Lerner sports | Includes
    bibliographical references and index. | Audience: Ages 7–11 | Audience: Grades 4–6 | Summary: "Tom Brady and Joe
    Montana have won 11 combined Super Bowls. Fans agree that they are two of the greatest quarterbacks in football
    history. But which is the best? Compare their careers and find out"— Provided by publisher.
Identifiers: LCCN 2022033568 (print) | LCCN 2022033569 (ebook) | ISBN 9781728490847 (library binding) |
    ISBN 9781728495903 (ebook)
Subjects: LCSH: Brady, Tom, 1977–—Juvenile literature. | Montana, Joe, 1956–—Juvenile literature. | Quarterbacks
    (Football)—United States—Biography—Juvenile literature.
Classification: LCC GV939.B685 S735 2024  (print) | LCC GV939.B685  (ebook) | DDC 796.332092 [B]—dc23/eng/20220715

LC record available at https://lccn.loc.gov/2022033568
LC ebook record available at https://lccn.loc.gov/2022033569

Manufactured in the United States of America
1-53015-51033-12/27/2022

# TABLE OF CONTENTS

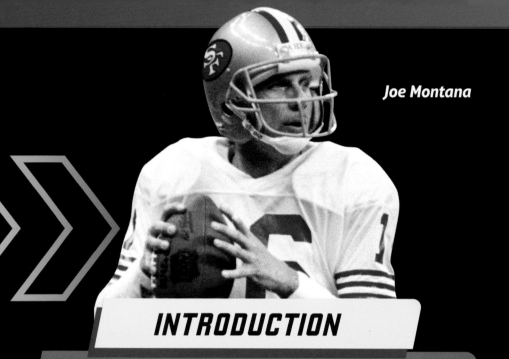

*Joe Montana*

## INTRODUCTION

# SUPER BOWL WINNERS

Quarterback Joe Montana won four Super Bowls with the San Francisco 49ers. But he may have saved his best for last. In January 1990, the 49ers faced the Denver Broncos in the National Football League (NFL) championship game.

## FAST FACTS

- Joe Montana is a three-time Super Bowl MVP.
- Montana is a member of the Pro Football Hall of Fame.
- Tom Brady won seven Super Bowls, six with the New England Patriots and one with the Tampa Bay Buccaneers.
- Brady led the NFL in touchdown passes five times.

Less than five minutes into the game, Montana threw a perfect pass over the middle of the field to wide receiver Jerry Rice. Rice snagged the ball out of the air and bounced off a Broncos defender. He raced into the end zone for a touchdown.

Montana's great throw was just the beginning. He completed 22 of 29 passes for 297 yards and five touchdowns. During one stretch, he completed 13 passes in a row and set a Super Bowl record. By the end of the game, Montana held several Super Bowl passing records. The 49ers won 55–10.

*Tom Brady*

For many fans, the 1990 Super Bowl was the greatest game of Montana's career. But was it the best Super Bowl performance ever? Let's look at what another quarterback did in the 2002 Super Bowl. The game was tied 17–17 with less than two minutes left in the game. Tom Brady led the New England Patriots down the field with a series of short, perfect passes. The long drive helped the Patriots kick a game-winning field goal. They won a last-second 20–17 victory over the St. Louis Rams.

The 2002 Super Bowl was the first of seven NFL championships for Brady—three more than Montana won. But does that make Brady the better quarterback? Or do Montana's records make him the better quarterback? Let's find out. Let the smackdown begin!

*Players, coaches, and many others celebrate on the field after the Patriots won the 2002 Super Bowl.*

Brady's seven Super Bowl wins are three more than any other quarterback has won.

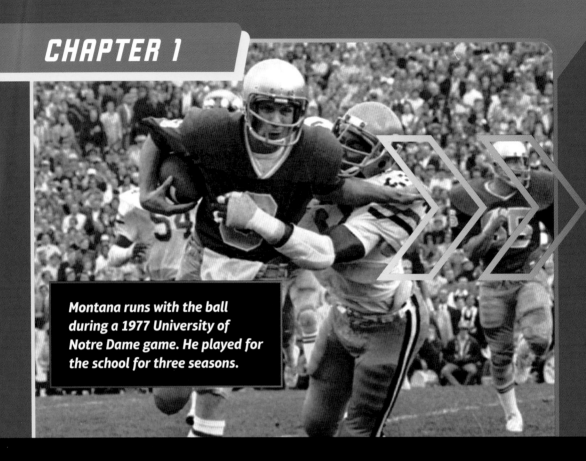

## CHAPTER 1

*Montana runs with the ball during a 1977 University of Notre Dame game. He played for the school for three seasons.*

# ROAD TO THE NFL

Joe Montana was born on June 11, 1956, in New Eagle, Pennsylvania. He grew up in the nearby town of Monongahela.

As a kid, Montana loved basketball and football. He played both sports in high school. He also sang in the school choir. Montana faced a decision. Two different colleges wanted him to play for them. North Carolina State University offered him a basketball scholarship. The University of Notre Dame offered him a football scholarship. Montana chose Notre Dame and football.

At Notre Dame, Montana was known for being cool under pressure. In a 1979 game in freezing weather in Dallas, Texas, Montana had a bad case of the flu. He led Notre Dame to victory after warming up with a bowl of chicken soup at halftime.

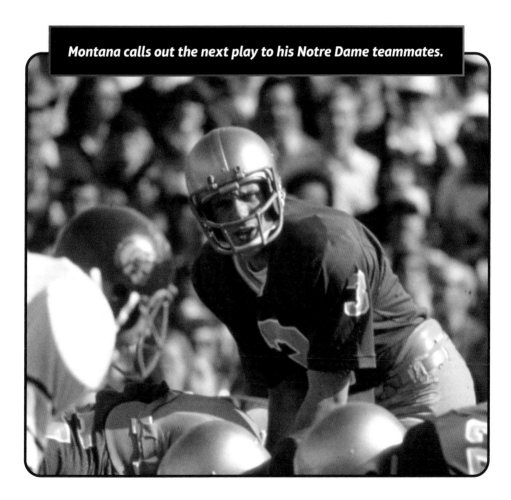

*Montana calls out the next play to his Notre Dame teammates.*

Even though he was the starting quarterback on a top college team, Montana was not a sure thing for the NFL. Some scouts thought he was too small for the league. In the 1979 NFL Draft, teams chose 81 players before the 49ers picked Montana. San Francisco's coach, Bill Walsh, thought Montana's strong, accurate arm made him a good fit for the 49ers. But almost nobody else thought Montana would become a star.

*Montana runs away from a University of Houston player at the 1979 Cotton Bowl. Notre Dame won the game 35–34.*

*Brady played for the University of Michigan Wolverines from 1996 to 1999.*

Tom Brady followed a similar path to the NFL. He was born in San Mateo, California, on August 3, 1977. Brady also played two sports. He was a high school baseball and football star. After high school, the Montreal Expos chose Brady in the 1995 Major League Baseball draft. But baseball wasn't his first choice. He decided to play college football instead.

When the University of Michigan offered Brady a football scholarship, he jumped at the chance. In his junior year, Brady became the team's starting quarterback. The next season, he led the Wolverines to a win in the Orange Bowl.

*Brady was a member of Michigan's football team for four seasons. But he mostly sat on the bench during the first two seasons.*

# CONSIDER THIS

Montana threw 25 touchdown passes in 27 games with Notre Dame. In 29 games with Michigan, Brady threw 30 touchdowns.

Like Montana, Brady hoped to be an early pick in the NFL Draft. But also like Montana, Brady had to wait. The Patriots chose Brady with the 199th overall pick in the 2000 draft. Since the Patriots already had an excellent quarterback in Drew Bledsoe, Brady would have to wait even longer for his chance to play.

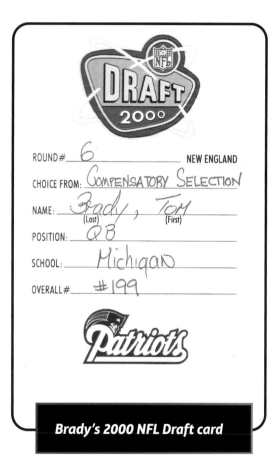

**Brady's 2000 NFL Draft card**

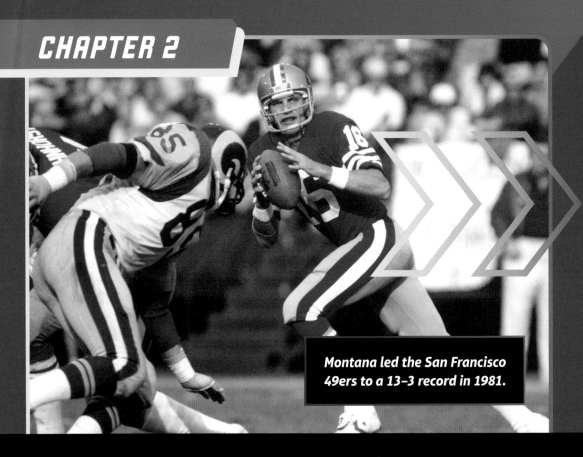

## CHAPTER 2

Montana led the San Francisco 49ers to a 13–3 record in 1981.

# GREAT MOMENTS

Joe Montana became the San Francisco 49ers starting quarterback midway through his second season. Soon he became one of the NFL's best. In his third year in the league, Montana led the 49ers to the playoffs.

San Francisco took on the Dallas Cowboys in the 1981 conference championship game. Most people expected the Cowboys to win. They led 27–21 with just under five minutes left in the game. Then Montana led the 49ers down the field with one of his classic comeback drives. With less than one minute to play, he made an off-balance pass to the back of the end zone. Teammate Dwight Clark snagged the ball with the tips of his fingers for the winning touchdown. Fans called it The Catch. The 49ers were headed to their first Super Bowl.

Montana stayed calm against a tough Dallas defense in the 1981 conference championship.

*Dwight Clark spikes the ball in celebration after making his famous touchdown catch.*

The 49ers won the Super Bowl, beating the Cincinnati Bengals 26–21. Montana earned the first of his three Super Bowl MVP awards. Seven years later, Montana faced the Bengals again with the championship on the line. Cincinnati led by three with just over three minutes to play. Montana was cool as always. Throwing pinpoint passes, he led San Francisco down the field. From the Cincinnati 10-yard line,

he passed to wide receiver John Taylor for the winning score.
Many people said it was the greatest drive in Super Bowl
history. The 49ers were Super Bowl champs again, 20–16.

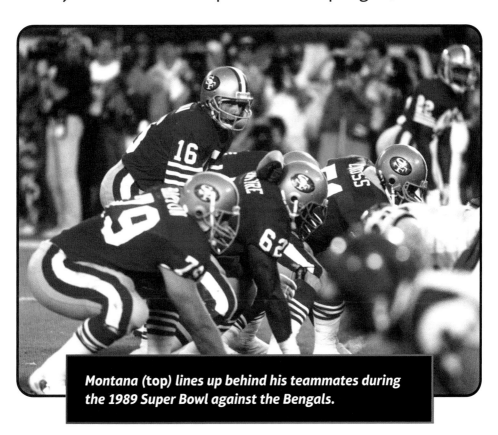

*Montana (top) lines up behind his teammates during
the 1989 Super Bowl against the Bengals.*

Tom Brady did not have to wait as long for his first NFL title. After replacing an injured Bledsoe early in the season, Brady led the Patriots to the 2002 Super Bowl. Their last-second win over the fast and powerful St. Louis Rams and their amazing offense—known as the Greatest Show on Turf—was one of the most surprising wins in Super Bowl history.

*Colorful confetti rains down on Brady and the Patriots after their win in the 2002 Super Bowl.*

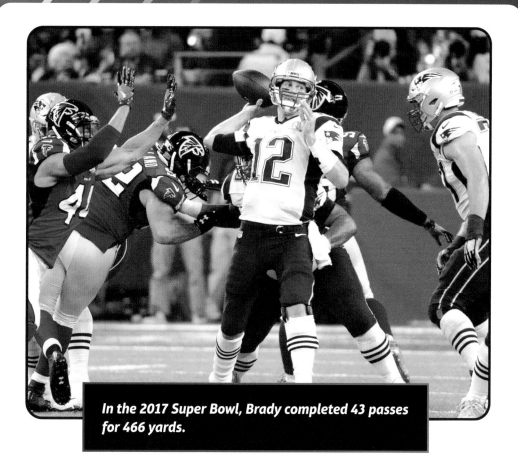

In the 2017 Super Bowl, Brady completed 43 passes for 466 yards.

Brady also led the greatest comeback in Super Bowl history. In 2017, the Atlanta Falcons led New England by 25 points in the third quarter. Some fans began to leave their seats, sure that the Falcons would win. But Brady refused to quit. He led the Patriots on a furious comeback that ended with a 91-yard drive to tie the game. Then, in overtime, he completed five straight passes to bring New England close to the end zone. Running back James White's touchdown sealed the win. Brady earned his fourth Super Bowl MVP award.

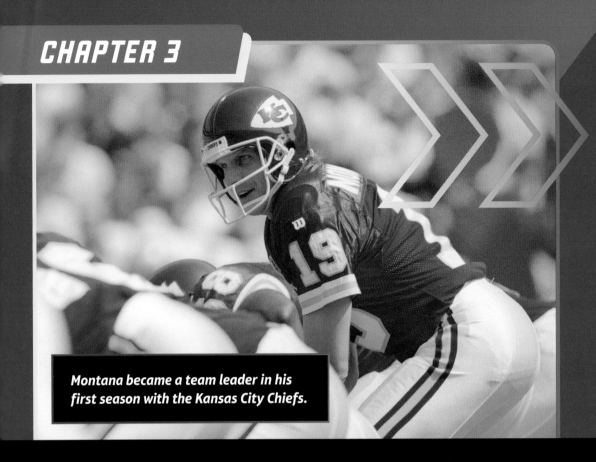

## CHAPTER 3

Montana became a team leader in his first season with the Kansas City Chiefs.

# PASSING BY THE NUMBERS

Montana and Brady are both big-game quarterbacks. They play their best when their teams need them most. Brady won the NFL MVP award three times. Montana won the award twice. Both Brady and Montana left their original teams and had success with new teams. Montana left the 49ers for the Kansas City Chiefs and led them to the playoffs. Brady left the Patriots for the Tampa Bay Buccaneers and won the 2021 Super Bowl.

During his career, Montana led his teams to 34 fourth-quarter comeback victories. He won four Super Bowls. Montana was also the first player to win three Super Bowl MVP awards.

Montana completed 3,409 career passes for 40,551 yards. He threw 273 touchdowns. He also rushed for 1,676 yards and 20 touchdowns. Always cool under pressure, nobody was better with a loud crowd rooting against them than Montana.

Montana's 273 career touchdown passes ranked 19th in NFL history after the 2022 season.

He holds the NFL quarterback record for most road wins in a row with 18. When NFL Network released its list of greatest players of all time, Montana was number four. He joined the Pro Football Hall of Fame in 2000.

*Montana with a statue of his likeness at the Pro Football Hall of Fame*

*Brady is one of the most accurate passers in NFL history. He rarely missed his target.*

Tom Brady holds nearly every quarterback record. He has the most career wins, passing touchdowns, and passing yards. He won his first 10 playoff games and led the Patriots to their first unbeaten season. The 2007 Patriots had a perfect 16–0 regular season record that no other NFL team has matched. He was a master at the fourth-quarter comeback. Brady led his teams on 14 game-winning drives in the playoffs. That's more than double any other quarterback's total. He retired from the NFL after the 2022 season and will soon join the Pro Football Hall of Fame.

## CHAPTER 4

Brady celebrates another touchdown pass with the Buccaneers.

# AND THE WINNER IS

Who is the winner of this all-star quarterback smackdown? You can decide for yourself. Brady and Montana are both all-time great quarterbacks, so there is no right or wrong answer. Different people may have different opinions. That's part of the fun of being a sports fan.

So, who do you think is best? Let's consider a few more things. Brady has the edge over Montana in Super Bowl wins. Brady won seven Super Bowls to Montana's four. But Montana never lost a Super Bowl, while Brady lost the big game three times. Does that make Montana a better big-game quarterback?

Left to right: *Head coach Bill Walsh, Montana, and 49ers owner Edward Debartolo Jr. with the 1985 Super Bowl trophy*

Stats such as passing yards favor Brady. But Brady played eight more seasons, and threw many more passes, than Montana did. If Montana had played as many seasons as Brady did, would their numbers match up?

Montana played in the 1980s, when quarterbacks did not pass as much as they do in the modern NFL. He set many records that were later broken by quarterbacks who passed a lot more often—and threw more touchdowns—than he did. If Montana played today, his numbers might be even better.

Based on the stats and the number of Super Bowl wins, Tom Brady is the winner of this smackdown. Who do you think the winner is? Think it over and make your choice!

*Would Montana have been even better if he played today?*

No other quarterback can match Brady's records and Super Bowl wins.

### JOE MONTANA

Date of birth: June 11, 1956
Height: 6 feet 2 (1.9 m)
Super Bowl wins: 4
Super Bowl MVP awards: 3
NFL MVP awards: 2

## TOM BRADY

Date of birth: August 3, 1977
Height: 6 feet 4 (1.9 m)
Super Bowl wins: 7
Super Bowl MVP awards: 5
NFL MVP awards: 3

# GLOSSARY

**conference:** a group of sports teams. The NFL has two conferences, the American Football Conference and the National Football Conference.

**comeback:** a win after being behind in a game

**draft:** when teams take turns choosing new players

**drive:** a series of football plays

**end zone:** the area at each end of a football field where players score touchdowns

**field goal:** a score of three points made by kicking the ball over the crossbar

**interception:** a pass caught by the other team that results in a change in possession

**MVP:** short for most valuable player

**scholarship:** money that a student receives to help pay for school

**scout:** a person who judges the skills of athletes

**Super Bowl:** the NFL's championship game

**wide receiver:** a football player whose main job is to catch passes

# LEARN MORE

Abdo, Kenny. *Tom Brady*. Minneapolis: Fly!, 2022.

American Football Facts for Kids
https://kids.kiddle.co/American_football

Joe Montana: Pro Football Hall of Fame
https://www.profootballhof.com/players/joe-montana/

Levit, Joe. *Meet Tom Brady*. Minneapolis: Lerner Publications, 2023.

Lowe, Alexander. *G.O.A.T. Football Quarterbacks*. Minneapolis: Lerner Publications, 2023.

*Sports Illustrated Kids*: Football
https://www.sikids.com/football

# INDEX

# PHOTO ACKNOWLEDGMENTS

Image credits: wavebreakmedia/Shutterstock, p. 2; NewsBase/AP Images, p. 4; Paul Spinelli/AP Images, pp. 5, 12; Ronald Martinez/Getty Images, p. 6; Jon Soohoo/Getty Images, p. 7; FHJ/AP Images, p. 8; Tony Tomsic/AP Images, p. 9; Bettmann/Getty Images, p. 10; Scott Boehm/AP Images, p. 11; Pro Football Hall of Fame/AP Images, p. 13; Peter Read Miller/AP Images, pp. 14, 17; Arthur Anderson/AP Images, p. 15; Al Messerschmidt/AP Images, p. 16; JEFF HAYNES/AFP/Getty Images, p. 18; Focus on Sport/Getty Images, pp. 19, 28; Mike Powell/Allsport/Getty Images, p. 20; Rich Pilling/Diamond Images/Getty Images, p. 21; DAVID MAXWELL/AFP/Getty Images, p. 22; Chris Graythen/Getty Images, pp. 23, 24; File/AP Images, p. 25; Otto Gruele Jr/Allsport/Getty Images, p. 26; Cliff Welch/Icon Sportswire/Getty Images, p. 27; Jim McIsaac/Getty Images, p. 29.

Cover: Jason Behnken/AP Images (Tom Brady); Otto Greule Jr/Getty Images (Joe Montana).